NEURODIVERGENT LEGENDS
WHO CHANGED THE WORLD

Caissie Dillon

© 2026 Neurodivergent Legends Pty Ltd. All rights reserved.
No part of this publication may be reproduced, stored in a retrieval system, or transmitted in any form or by any means (electronic, mechanical, photocopying, recording, or otherwise) without prior written permission from the publisher, except in the case of brief quotations embodied in critical articles or reviews.

Published by Neurodivergent Legends Pty Ltd
Melbourne, Australia
Author: Caissie Dillon
Cover Design & Illustrations: Caissie Dillon

ISBN: 978-1-7644400-0-4

This book is a work of nonfiction created to inspire, educate, and celebrate neurodivergent individuals. All biographical information is based on publicly available sources. Any unintentional errors will be corrected in subsequent editions.

Everybody is a genius.
But if you judge a fish by its ability to climb a tree,
it will live its whole life believing that it is stupid.

Albert Einstein

ALBERT EINSTEIN   02
The Scientist Who Taught the World to Wonder

SIMONE BILES   06
The Gymnast Who Defied Gravity

STEVE JOBS   10
The Creator Who Changed How We Connect

EMILY DICKINSON   14
The Quiet Poet Who Lived Between the Lines

THOMAS EDISON   18
The Inventor Who Created the Future

BILLIE EILISH   22
The Singer Who Felt the World Differently

RICHARD BRANSON   26
The Risk-Taker Who Built a Global Empire

WINSTON CHURCHILL   30
The Leader Who Became a Voice in the Dark

STEPHEN HAWKING   34
The Mind That Travelled Beyond the Stars

MICHAEL JORDAN   38
The Athlete Who Lived in the Air

TEMPLE GRANDIN   42
The Scientist Who Listened to Animals

FRIDA KAHLO   46
The Artist Who Turned Pain into Colour

ALAN TURING   50
The Mathematician Who Helped End the War

MUHAMMAD ALI   54
The Champion Who Redefined Greatness

GRETA THUNBERG   58
The Young Voice Who Refused to Look Away

LEONARDO DA VINCI   62
The Genius Who Sketched the Future

WHOOPI GOLDBERG   66
The Star Who Found Her Voice on Stage

ISAAC NEWTON   70
The Thinker Who Made Sense of the Universe

STEVEN SPIELBERG   74
The Director Who Saw Stories Everywhere

MARIE CURIE   78
The Scientist Who Studied in Secret

PABLO PICASSO   82
The Artist Who Changed Reality

AGATHA CHRISTIE   86
The Writer Who Turned Silence into Suspense

Albert Einstein

~ THE SCIENTIST WHO TAUGHT THE WORLD TO WONDER ~

Albert Einstein learned early
that the world loved answers.
Quick ones.
Clean ones.
The kind you could circle in pencil
and move on.

But Albert wasn't built that way.

At school, others raced ahead
to find the answer,
Albert slowed down.
Paused.
Let the question stretch its legs.
Let it breathe.
Listened for what it hadn't said yet.

He stared out windows
longer than expected.
Let his mind drift like a paper boat
on a wide, curious river.

Questions led to more questions.

Why?
Why this?
Why not that?

Students sniggered.
Teachers sighed.
Why was he always behind?

But Albert wasn't behind.
He was somewhere else entirely.

Inside his mind,
thoughts appeared as shapes,
colours,
motion.
Not words marching in rows,
but detailed scenes unfolding.

He imagined light
as something you could chase.
Time as something that could bend.
Space as a thing that could stretch,
like fabric pulled gently,
then changed forever.

He asked questions
that didn't fit neatly on the page.
Questions without clear edges.
Questions that refused to sit still.

And he stayed with them.
Long after the bell rang.
Long after others were done.
Long after the room emptied.

Years passed.
Albert grew up.
But he never stopped wondering.

He followed his questions into libraries,
into classrooms,
into late nights where silence felt loud
and thinking felt alive.

He discovered that time
doesn't tick the same for everyone.
That space can curve.

Albert Einstein learned early
that the world loved answers.
Quick ones.
Clean ones.
The kind you could circle in pencil
and move on.

But Albert wasn't built that way.

At school, others raced ahead
to find the answer.
Albert slowed down.
Paused.
Let the question stretch its legs.
Let it breathe.
Listened for what it hadn't said yet.

He stared out windows
longer than expected.
Let his mind drift like a paper boat
on a wide, curious river.

Questions led to more questions.

Why?
Why this?
Why not that?

Students sniggered.
Teachers sighed.
Why was he always behind?

But Albert wasn't behind.
He was somewhere else entirely.

Simone Biles

~ THE GYMNAST WHO DEFIED GRAVITY ~

Simone Biles's routines were so daring,
the rulebook had to catch up.
Four skills carry her name.
Moves no one else had ever landed.

She didn't just master gymnastics.
She expanded it.

But before the medals,
before the history,
Simone was a kid with too much energy
for small spaces.

Sitting still felt impossible.
Her thoughts ran ahead.
Her body needed motion
the way lungs need air.

Simone is neurodivergent.
She has ADHD.
Not a lack of focus,
but focus that moves.
A mind that reacts fast.
Creates fast.

In classrooms, lessons dragged.
Instructions blurred.
Stillness was demanded
from a body built to move.

Teachers grew frustrated.
But Simone wasn't broken.
She was misread.

The gym told a different story.
Movement wasn't the problem.
It was the answer.

Restlessness became power.
Fast thoughts became split-second decisions.
Energy sharpened into control.

She trained relentlessly.
Routine after routine.
Again.
Again.

ADHD hyperfocus took over.
Muscle learned what the mind imagined.

Simone's mind moves fast.
Her body moves faster.
Thought and motion arrive together.
No pause between intention and action.

Precision lives in her bones.
Energy hums beneath her skin.
She feels everything.
Balance.
Pressure.
The slightest shift
that could change everything.

By 2016, the world was watching.
At the Rio Olympics,
Simone won four gold medals.

Her confidence was electric.
Her joy unmistakable.
The world called her fearless.
Invincible.

Simone knew better.

She knew that strength
is not the absence of fear.
It's the presence of honesty.

When her private medical information was leaked,
the world learned she had ADHD.
That she took prescribed medication.

Simone didn't flinch.

"I have ADHD, and it is nothing to be ashamed of."

She told the world that
ADHD doesn't limit talent.
It can sharpen it.
Strengthen it.
Lift it higher.

ADHD is energy.
Intensity.
Passion without a dimmer switch.

When supported,
when understood,
it becomes brilliance.

So if your thoughts move fast…
If your energy feels big…
If your focus ignites when you're doing what you love…
Think of Simone Biles.

She flew higher than anyone before her.
Then showed us all how powerful it is
to land safely inside yourself.

Steve Jobs

~ THE CREATOR WHO CHANGED HOW WE CONNECT ~

Steve Jobs' mind leapt ahead of him.
Ideas didn't knock quietly.
They arrived all at once.
Loud.
Insistent.

When something caught his attention,
everything else vanished.
Noise thinned.
Time slipped its grip.
Focus came in waves.
Strong, sudden, unstoppable.
All or nothing.

Steve felt everything intensely.
Joy.
Frustration.
Beauty.
Disappointment.

School wasn't built for a mind like his.
Lessons crawled.
His thoughts sprinted.

He was bored.
Restless.
Misunderstood.
Told to behave.
Focus.
Calm down.
But Steve wasn't built for calm.

Classrooms couldn't hold him.
But the world outside could.

Then he met Steve Wozniak.
A builder.
An engineer.
Someone who loved making things
just to see if they could be made.

In a small California garage,
they began to build.
Not just tools.
Possibility.

They called it Apple.

Wozniak built the products.
Steve shaped the vision.

He believed technology should feel human.
That devices should listen.
That tools should disappear into your hands
and let your imagination take over.

Steve was demanding.
Often difficult.
He pushed people hard
because he could see
what something *could be*
before it existed at all.

He obsessed over every detail.
The curve of an edge.
The weight of a device in the hand.
The sound of a click.

That obsession changed everything.
The iPod.
The iPhone.

The iPad.
The Mac.

He didn't just build devices.
He built experiences.
A way to hold music.
A way to touch ideas.
A way to carry the world
in your pocket.

People called him a visionary.
A genius.
A disruptor.

But at heart,
Steve Jobs was a questioner.
Someone who never stopped asking:
Why not better?

He once said,

"Stay hungry. Stay foolish."

He meant:
Don't get comfortable.
Don't stop wondering.

So if your emotions feel too big…
If you don't fit the system…
If your ideas arrive before others are ready…
Think of Steve Jobs.

He chose vision over approval.
Curiosity over calm.
And by trusting the leap inside his mind,
he helped the world leap forward too.

Emily Dickinson

~ THE QUIET POET WHO LIVED
BETWEEN THE LINES ~

Emily Dickinson noticed everything.
Light sliding across the floor.
Bees revising the air.
The small hush between raindrops.

She preferred being alone.
Solitude felt safe.
Ordered.
Clear.

From her room,
Emily built a universe.
One window.
One desk.
One white dress.
And a mind that travelled everywhere.

Emily lived in the 1800s,
before there were names
for a mind like hers.
But her way of being
told the story anyway.

She loved routine.
Familiar patterns.
Steady rhythms.
Social rules confused her.
Noise pressed too hard.
Too close.

That sensitivity sharpened her sight.
What overwhelmed others
became her instrument.

Emily poured her inner world into poetry.
Small poems.
Exact poems.
Poems that captured truth
without explaining it away.

She wrote of death as if it were a polite visitor.
Of hope as a stubborn thing with feathers.
Of pain as something sharp and honest
that deserved to be named.

Emily used dashes
the way others used breath.
To pause.
To pivot.
To leave space
for the reader
to arrive on their own.

She didn't rush meaning.
Didn't smooth the edges.
She let ambiguity live.
Let truth flicker instead of shout.

Emily wrote nearly 1,800 poems.
Yet she chose privacy over publication.
Editors wanted to tidy her lines.
Make her sound like everyone else.

Emily refused.
Her words were precise.
To change them was to change the truth.

When Emily died,
her sister Lavinia found the poems.
Hundreds of them.

A lifetime of creation
waiting quietly
to be discovered.

The world finally caught up.
Read her words.
Learned that restraint can be power.
That softness can be strength.
That staying small
does not mean thinking small.

Emily once wrote,

"I dwell in possibility."

And she meant it.

She lived there.
Built a home inside it.
Left the door ajar
for anyone brave enough
to step through.

So if noise overwhelms you…
If solitude feels like oxygen…
If you notice details others rush past…
Think of Emily Dickinson.

She didn't need the world
to come to her.
She listened closely.
Wrote honestly.
And proved that a quiet life
can echo forever.

Thomas Edison

~ THE INVENTOR WHO CREATED THE FUTURE ~

Thomas Edison's mind was a room
with every light switched on at once.
Ideas flickered.
Popped.
Sparked.

School felt wrong.
Too slow.
Too quiet.
Lessons crawled
while his thoughts
sprinted ahead.

Questions spilled out.
Why does this work?
What if it didn't?
What happens when it breaks?

Teachers ran out of answers.

Thomas' imagination was limitless.
His determination was relentless.

When something caught his interest,
the world vanished.
Hours slipped past.
Days blurred.
Focus locked in tight.

In Thomas' time there were no words
for learning differences.

Only judgement.
Only labels.

At home, his mother listened.
She didn't try to dim him.
She gave him books.
Tools.
Time.

The basement became a laboratory.
Curiosity finally had room to breathe.
Imagination had space to stretch.

He learned by doing.
By touching.
By breaking things just to see
how they worked.

He didn't want answers handed to him.
He wanted to *discover* them.

His attention turned to invention.
The phonograph.
Motion pictures.
Sound captured forever.
Light pulled from darkness.

But none of it came easy.

Thomas failed constantly.
Experiments fizzled.
Ideas collapsed.
Materials burned out.
Again.
And again.
And again.

Thousands of tries for one right light filament.
People laughed.
They told him to quit.

Thomas refused.

He didn't call it failure.
He called it information.
Each mistake taught him something.
Each try narrowed the path.

He famously said,

**"I have not failed.
I have just found 10,000 ways that will not work."**

That is how Thomas Edison
changed the world.

Not by getting it right the first time.
But by refusing to stop
when others would.

So if you fail again and again…
If learning seems different for you…
If you question things more than find answers…
Think of Thomas Edison.

He proved that brilliance
isn't about perfection.
It's about curiosity.
Persistence.

And the courage to keep going.
Even when the light
hasn't turned on
yet.

Billie Eilish

~ THE SINGER WHO FELT THE
WORLD DIFFERENTLY ~

Billie Eilish could feel sound.

In her bones.
In her skin.
In her nervous system.

Not just the noise.
The feelings
underneath it.

The hum of anxiety.
The buzz of too much.
The echo of being watched.

Her mind was loud.
Sensitive.
Wide open.

Crowded rooms pressed in.
Bright lights shouted.
Expectations scraped.

Billie is neurodivergent.
She has Tourette syndrome.

Her body reacts
before she can explain.
A blink.
A twitch.
A sound she can't stop.

But Billie didn't hide from the noise.

She turned it
into music.

At home,
with her brother,
beats bloomed in a bedroom.

Lyrics spilled like secrets.
Melodies moved slow,
then sharp,
then soft again.

She sang the way she felt.
Quiet when the world screamed.
Raw when the world pretended.

Her voice didn't beg for attention.
It invited you closer.

But those same sensitivities,
that deep noticing,
that emotional volume,
became her superpower.

She didn't sing like everyone else.
She didn't dress for approval.
She didn't smile on cue.

She chose comfort.
Control.
Honesty.

Whispers over shouting.
Truth over polish.
Feeling over perfection.

Awards followed.
Crowds grew.
Stages stretched bigger,
brighter.

But Billie stayed herself.

Still listening.
Still feeling.
Still turning vulnerability
into art.

As her platform grew,
Billie spoke openly
about being neurodivergent.
She explained her tics.
Didn't hide them.

She showed the world
that difference
doesn't need covering up.
It needs understanding.

She once said,

"You don't need to be perfect to be amazing."

So if your body moves unexpectedly...
If your feelings feel loud...
If the world feels too much...
Think of Billie Eilish.

She didn't silence her differences.
She made them sing.

Richard Branson

~ THE RISK TAKER WHO BUILT A GLOBAL EMPIRE ~

Richard Branson didn't shine in school.
School didn't shine for him either.
Teachers called him lazy.
Unfocused.
Some said he'd never amount to much.

Richard is neurodivergent.
He has dyslexia.

Words tangled on the page.
Spelling tests felt like traps.
Reading demanded time and focus
classrooms never gave.
Every lesson judged him.

Richard's mind was busy.
Full of ideas.
Imagination.
Possibility.

While others memorised facts,
Richard noticed patterns.
While students followed instructions,
he questioned them.
While they read quietly,
he imagined boldly.

He thought in big pictures.
Dreamed in bright colours.

He saw possibilities
where others saw rules.
Adventures where others saw risk.

Outside school,
creativity mattered more
than neat handwriting.
Ideas mattered more
than perfect spelling.

So at sixteen,
Richard left school.
Not to stop learning.
To learn differently.

He started a magazine.
Then a record business.
A recording studio.
Then an airline.

One idea led to the next.
Curiosity came first.
Certainty came later.

Where others hesitated,
he jumped.
Where others said *no*,
he asked *why not?*

Mistakes happened.
Big ones.
Expensive ones.

But Richard didn't quit.
He adjusted the sails.
Changed direction.
Kept moving.

He named his company Virgin
because he was new to business.
But he wasn't new to dreaming.

Business wasn't numbers to him.
It was people.
Stories.
Energy.

Again and again,
his ideas worked.

But Richard's impact
goes beyond business.

He speaks openly
about dyslexia.
About neurodivergence.

He tells young people
who struggle in school
to trust their minds.
To choose creativity
over conformity.
To see difference
as potential,
not limitation.

So if reading feels hard…
If school makes you doubt yourself…
If your mind is bursting with ideas…
Think of Richard Branson.

He stayed curious.
Kept asking questions.
Kept backing people.
He proved that difference
isn't weakness.
It's fuel.

Winston Churchill
~ THE LEADER WHO BECAME A VOICE IN THE DARK ~

Winston Churchill struggled in school.
Reading came slowly.
His handwriting tangled.
Sometimes even he couldn't read it.

Teachers called him careless.
Distracted.
Difficult.

Winston felt the weight of those words.
Carried them quietly.
Let them bruise,
but not break him.

Inside his mind,
ideas thundered.
Images collided.
Thoughts raced like storms
searching for somewhere to land.

Winston learned something early:
if his thoughts came fast and fierce,
his words would have to be shaped with care.

He didn't write quickly.
He wrote deliberately.
Slowly.
Again and again.

He dictated.
Spoke sentences aloud.
Tested their rhythm.
Their weight.
Their truth.

Language became his weapon.
His refuge.
His way through.

Winston was sensitive.
Emotional.
Deeply affected by failure.
By rejection.
By the ache of not fitting
where he was expected to belong.

That sensitivity built something powerful:
An inner world that was bold.
Vivid.
Restless.
And under pressure,
his mind didn't freeze.
It ignited.

As a young man,
Winston searched for intensity.
He joined the army.
Travelled through war zones.

He noticed patterns early.
Felt danger before others would name it.
He warned of threats no one else saw.

For years he was ignored.
Dismissed.
Criticised.

Then history shifted.

In 1939, war engulfed Europe.
Cities burned.
Fear spread.

The future felt fragile.
Uncertain.

And when the world stood in the dark,
Winston Churchill stepped forward to lead.

The same mind once dismissed in classrooms
now steadied a nation.

His intensity became clarity.
His emotional depth became conviction.
His sensitivity became strength.

He once said,

**"Success is not final. Failure is not fatal.
It is the courage to continue that counts."**

Winston Churchill didn't conquer fear
by pretending it wasn't there.

He named it.
Spoke to it.
Walked through it,
sentence by sentence.

So if learning feels harder for you…
If words come out sideways…
If your mind carries both brilliance and weight…
Think of Winston Churchill.

The boy who struggled to read,
the man who battled his mind,
became the thinker who turned difference
into direction.

Stephen Hawking

~ THE MIND THAT TRAVELLED BEYOND THE STARS ~

Stephen Hawking's mind
was always reaching outward.
Past the edge of the page.
Past the edge of the sky.

He didn't just wonder what was.
He wondered why.

Why stars burned instead of fading out.
Why time moved forward and never back.
Why space kept stretching,
as if the universe itself were curious.

Stephen noticed patterns early.
Order.
Logic.
Structure.

Social rules felt awkward.
Conversation felt slow.
But systems made sense.
Numbers made sense.
The universe made sense.

At university, his curiosity caught fire.
Physics.
Mathematics.
Cosmology.
Big questions with no ceilings.

At twenty-one, his body changed the rules.
Stephen was diagnosed with ALS.

Doctors gave him a short future.

Time grew loud.
Fragile.
Urgent.

But instead of shrinking his questions,
Stephen widened them.

As his body lost motion,
his thinking gained speed.
Distractions fell away.
Focus remained.

His mind travelled where his body could not.
Into black holes.
Into the beginning of time.
Into places where space bends
and certainty breaks.

As the disease progressed,
Stephen used a wheelchair.

When he lost his voice,
he spoke through a machine.
The sound was quiet,
but the ideas were not.

He showed that black holes are not silent.
That they glow.
That they leak energy.

Stephen used equations
the way poets use metaphor.
Dense.
Precise.
Elegant.

His book, *A Brief History of Time*,
reached millions.
He somehow made the universe
feel both vast
and personal.

He invited everyone,
not just scientists,
to wonder.

He once said,

> **"Remember to look up at the stars
> and not down at your feet."**

Stephen lived far longer than expected.
He married.
Became a father.
A teacher.
A challenger of limits.

So if you ever feel confined…
If your body or mind works differently…
If your voice takes a different path…
Think of Stephen Hawking.

He proved that brilliance
is not measured by movement.
That imagination outruns muscle.

And a determined mind
can travel farther than the stars.

Michael Jordan

~ THE ATHLETE WHO LIVED
IN THE AIR ~

Michael Jordan's energy never sat still.
It paced.
Bounced.
Waited for somewhere to go.

As a kid, he moved before thinking.
Thought before finishing.
Competition lived in his bones.
Stillness felt like holding your breath too long.

School asked him to sit still.
Slow down.

Basketball asked him to explode.

As a teenager,
Michael wasn't the tallest.
Wasn't the strongest.
Wasn't handed anything early.

He was cut from his high school varsity team.
Sent back to the junior squad.
Told he wasn't ready.

He went home angry.
Hurt.
Fuelled.

Instead of shrinking,
he trained.
Before school.
After dinner.
After everyone else stopped watching.
Until the driveway lights clicked off.

Until repetition replaced doubt.
Until sweat rewrote the story.

On the court, the noise inside him sharpened.
Restlessness became rhythm.
Chaos learned direction.
Energy turned into precision.

The faster the game moved,
the clearer his mind became.

His focus came in hot.
All-consuming.
Unavoidable.

Crowds disappeared.
Time bent.
The court narrowed
to instinct and air.

Michael jumped
like gravity had blinked.
Hung where defenders couldn't reach.
Twisted mid-flight,
deciding after leaving the ground
how the story would end.

Michael became known as the GOAT.
Six NBA championships.
Five MVP awards.
Fourteen All-Star selections.

But numbers were never the point.

His true legacy lived in the mindset.
The refusal to coast.
The refusal to soften.

The decision to try again
even when failure already knew his name.

Michael once said,

> "I can accept failure.
> Everyone fails at something.
> But I can't accept not trying."

He didn't escape his intensity.
He trained it.
Directed it.
Let it lift him higher than caution ever could.

He showed the world
that greatness isn't perfection.
It's hunger.
Relentless drive.
And the courage to rise again,
and again,
and again.

So if your energy feels too big...
If criticism sticks longer than it should...
If competition lights something fierce inside you...
Think of Michael Jordan.

He couldn't sit still
because he was never meant to.
Every restless movement was preparation.
Every surge of energy was practice.

He wasn't learning how to fit in.
He was learning how to fly.

Temple Grandin

~ THE SCIENTIST WHO LISTENED TO ANIMALS ~

For Temple Grandin,
the world felt loud.
Like it had forgotten
how to whisper.

Lights buzzed.
Voices crashed.
Crowds felt like storms
with no shelter.

Temple didn't like hugs.
Didn't like surprises.
Didn't like chaos
she couldn't map.

People said she was strange.
Too quiet.
Too blunt.
Too much herself.

They said,
She'll never live independently.
She'll never succeed.
She'll never understand the world.

Temple is autistic.

She wasn't confused.
She was tuned differently.

While others talked,
Temple noticed details.
While others guessed,
Temple observed.

The flick of a cow's ear.
A tightening of muscle.
A slight pause before panic.

Animals didn't use words.
They spoke through movement.
Through space.
Through feeling.

This silent language
felt familiar.

Temple began studying animal behaviour.
How fear travels through a body.
How stress changes movement.
How confusion creates pain.

And she realised something important.

Animals weren't difficult.
They weren't stubborn.
They weren't broken.

They were responding honestly
to environments that frightened them.
Confused them.
Overwhelmed them.

Bright lights.
Clanging metal.
Sharp turns.
Crowded spaces.

So Temple redesigned the systems.

Curved pathways
replaced sharp corners.

Harsh lights softened.
Visual distractions disappeared.

And something incredible happened.

Animals were calmer.
Safer.
So were the people
working with them.

Temple became a scientist.
A professor.
A writer.

She showed that autism isn't something to fix.
It is a different way of seeing.
One filled with precision.
Insight.
And deep empathy.

She helped parents understand their children.
Teachers understand their students.
She gave words to experiences
that never had language before.

So if your mind runs on images instead of words…
If noise feels louder to you…
If details pull your focus like magnets…
Think of Temple Grandin.

Her designs transformed the livestock industry.
Today, her work is used around the world.

Temple saw what others overlooked.
And because of that, millions of animals
now live calmer, more humane lives.

Frida Kahlo

~ THE ARTIST WHO TURNED
PAIN INTO COLOUR ~

Frida Kahlo felt everything intensely.
Beauty struck like lightning.
Joy arrived bright and sudden.
Sorrow settled deep in her bones.

Frida was deeply sensitive to her surroundings.
Noise.
Texture.
Colour.
Emotion.
Everything landed with force.

As a child, Frida spent long hours alone.
Not lonely.
Observant.

She drew.
She watched.
She imagined.

The curve of a leaf.
A shadow sliding across a wall.
Colours changing with the light.

Her mind translated images into feeling.
And feeling into images.

At eighteen, Frida's life changed forever.
A bus accident broke her body.
Her spine.
Her future.

Pain became constant.
Stillness became her world.

Confined to her bed,
she began to paint.
A mirror was placed above her.
A canvas rested within reach.

From that small, painful space,
Frida created entire worlds.

She painted what she knew best.
Her body.
Her heartbreak.
Her truth.

Pain became visible.
Emotion took shape.
Truth exploded in colour.

Frida didn't follow artistic rules.
She blended realism with imagination.
Dream with memory.
Symbol with self.

She painted herself again and again.
Not out of vanity.
But out of necessity.

Through her self-portraits,
Frida explored who she was.

Her heritage.
Her disability.
Her joy.

Her grief.

She dressed in vibrant colours.
Traditional Mexican clothing.

She celebrated her culture with pride.
She turned her body into art.
Her life into a statement.

Frida ignored the limits placed on her.
As a woman.
As a disabled person.
As someone who felt too much.

She refused to shrink.

Today, her work hangs in museums.
Her face is a symbol of honesty.
Resilience.
Self-expression.

But her legacy is deeper than fame.
She showed that pain can become power.
Difference can become beauty.

And truth,
expressed boldly,
can outlive the body that carried it.

So if your feelings run deep…
If your body tells stories before words do…
If your truth refuses to stay quiet…
Think of Frida Kahlo.

Her body carried limits.
Her spirit never did.
And her mind painted a legacy
the world will never forget.

Alan Turing

~ THE MATHEMATICIAN WHO HELPED END THE WAR ~

Alan Turing's mind was wired for precision.
Tuned for logic.
He noticed order where others saw mess.
Meaning inside patterns.
His curiosity was relentless.

Alan thought differently.
School misunderstood him.
Teachers overlooked him.
Classmates called him strange.

He avoided eye contact.
Found social rules confusing.
Casual conversations felt illogical.

So Alan kept to himself.
Kept thinking.
Kept problem-solving.

When World War II arrived,
Britain faced a terrifying challenge.
Germany was sending coded messages
using a machine called Enigma.

The code changed daily.
The possible combinations were vast.
Many believed it could never be broken.

At Bletchley Park,
a quiet place hiding enormous pressure,
Alan worked while the clock shouted.
Lives hung in the air.

Most people saw impossibility.
Alan saw structure.

Where panic lived,
Alan slowed down.
Where noise grew loud,
Alan's mind grew clear.

He approached the problem differently.
He trusted logic over guesswork.
Pattern over panic.

Working long hours,
often in near silence,
Alan designed a machine.

It tested possibilities faster than any
human mind ever could.
It did what no person alone could do.
It broke the Enigma code.

With that breakthrough,
the Allies could read enemy messages.
They could anticipate attacks.
Protect ships.
Save soldiers.

Alan's work helped shorten the war by years.
It saved millions of lives.
It quietly changed the course of history.

But history was not kind to Alan in return.

In a cruel twist of fate,
he was punished not for what he did,
but for who he loved.

At the time, it was a crime to love another man.
Alan was arrested.
Another tragic example of the world
misunderstanding differences.

Alan's mind worked differently.
His heart loved differently.
And instead of trying to understand either,
society chose control and cruelty.

After the war, Alan kept looking forward.
He began asking new questions.
Could machines think?
Could they learn?

Before artificial intelligence had a name,
Alan had imagined it.
Before the future arrived,
Alan built the door.

He once said,

**"Sometimes it is the people no one imagines anything
of who do the things that no one can imagine."**

So if you feel out of step…
If your thoughts move in patterns…
If your mind prefers truth over performance…
Think of Alan Turing.

The quiet mind.
The pattern-seer.
The thinker who helped end a war
and unknowingly began the digital age
simply by being exactly who he was.

Muhammad Ali

~ THE CHAMPION WHO REDEFINED GREATNESS ~

Before the world called him *The Greatest*,
he was Cassius Clay.
A kid from Louisville
with too much energy.

He talked fast.
Moved fast.
Thought fast.

Rhymes jumped out of him,
faster than teachers could catch it.
His memory lived in sound,
in cadence,
in beat.

School tried to slow him down.
Told him to sit still.
Read quietly.
Write neatly.

But he needed motion.
Challenge.
Urgency.
Purpose.

His mind was built for timing.
For instinct.
Expression.

Then, at twelve,
he found boxing.
He found his calling.

The gym gave his energy a shape.

The ring gave his thoughts a rhythm.
Gloves on.
Focus locked in.

Ali trained when others slept.
Ran when others rested.
But he didn't just fight with fists.
He fought with language.

He talked before the fight.
Not to entertain.
To own the moment.
To unsettle men before they moved.

Words became armour.
Rhythm became control.
Confidence became strategy.

He studied opponents closely.
Their confidence.
Their fear.

He sensed hesitation before it showed.
Predicted movement before it happened.

At twenty-two, he was heavyweight champion.
But titles weren't enough.
Ali was fighting for something bigger than belts.

He questioned the name he was given.
A name inherited through slavery,
a history that expected obedience.

He refused both
and decided who he wanted to be.
Muhammad Ali.

When he declared,

"I am the greatest."

He didn't say it to boast.
He said it to believe.
To claim confidence in a cruel world.

Then came his hardest fight.
He refused the Vietnam War draft.

They took the belt.
They took years.
They threatened prison.

But Ali didn't bend.
His values mattered more.

When he returned, time had marked him.
Speed had thinned.
But his mind had deepened.
He fought with angles now.
With patience.
With endurance.

He reclaimed the heavyweight title.
Fought battles that became legend.
Earned respect far beyond sport.

So if your thoughts race ahead…
If your body needs movement to think…
If your voice refuses to be quiet…
Think of Muhammad Ali.

He turned restless energy into discipline.
Words into power.
Belief into legacy.

Greta Thunberg

~ THE YOUNG VOICE WHO REFUSED TO LOOK AWAY ~

Greta Thunberg was eight years old,
when she learned about climate change.

It didn't pass through her mind.
It settled.
Pressed on her chest.
Refused to move.

The facts didn't whisper.
They shouted.
They asked questions that wouldn't sleep.

Why is no one acting?
Why are adults calm?
Why does the world keep going
like nothing is wrong?

Greta couldn't look away.
Her brain wouldn't let her.
Once something was true,
it stayed true.
Sharp.
Unsoftened.

The knowing became heavy.
Her anxiety grew loud.
She stopped eating.
Stopped speaking.
Her body carried the same urgency
her mind couldn't release.

Greta is neurodivergent.
She's spoken about her autism,

living with OCD,
her selective mutism.

Her mind processes truth literally.
Completely.
No blur.
No pause button.

Some called that a weakness.
Greta called it clarity.

As she grew, she found her voice.
Not loud.
Not dramatic.
Exact.

At fifteen, she sat outside Parliament.
One girl.
One sign.

School Strike for Climate.

Stillness became protest.
Silence echoed loud.

Photos spread.
Questions followed.
Other students joined her.

Soon, millions around the world
were striking for climate action.
Governments had to listen.
A global movement had begun.

Greta travelled across oceans.
She stood before presidents.
Prime ministers.

She addressed the United Nations.
Her words echoed far beyond the room.

She once said,

"No one is too small to make a difference."

Greta speaks with urgency,
unconcerned for comfort.
They called her too intense.
Too serious.

But Greta did not stop.

She told the world:
climate change is not a future problem.
It is happening now.
And silence is a choice.

Greta showed that young voices matter.
That neurodivergent minds see what others overlook.
That caring deeply isn't a flaw.
It is a responsibility.

So if you've been told you care too much…
If injustice weighs on your body…
If your intensity makes others uncomfortable…
Think of Greta Thunberg.

She refused to look away.
She turned concern into action.
Truth into movement.

She proved that one clear,
honest voice can change the world.

Leonardo da Vinci

~ THE GENIUS WHO SKETCHED THE FUTURE ~

Leonardo da Vinci's curiosity
was as divergent as his mind.
One moment, he was painting.
The next, studying anatomy.
Engineering.
Astronomy.

Where others saw a bird,
Leonardo saw a question.
How does it rise?
How does air hold weight?
How does flight begin?

He studied wings.
Measured feathers.
Tracked the wind with his eyes.

Imagined humans
lifting off the ground
centuries before anyone
believed it possible.

Where others saw a river,
Leonardo saw motion.
Currents folding into themselves.
Patterns repeating purposefully.

Where others saw a smile,
Leonardo looked behind it.
What muscles pull it upward?
What tension hides beneath it?
What truth lives behind the eyes?

Leonardo wrote backwards.
Struggled with spelling.
Left projects unfinished.

Most people know him as a painter.
The *Mona Lisa*.
The Last Supper.
But painting was only one language he spoke.

Leonardo was a scientist.
An engineer.
An architect.
An inventor.
A philosopher.

He sketched machines
the world wasn't ready for.
Flying devices.
Parachutes.
Submarines.
Ideas waiting patiently
for the future to catch up.

He studied the human body.
Bone.
Muscle.
Organ.

He treated anatomy
as both science and art.
Every line mattered.
Every structure told a story.

His notebooks overflowed.
Thousands of pages.

Drawings.
Diagrams.
Ideas.

Not always answers.
But always questions.

People grew frustrated with him.
They wanted finished work.
Clear answers.
One path.
Leonardo gave them something better.

Curiosity.

His art fed science.
Science fed invention.
Observation fed imagination.

He once said,

"Learning never exhausts the mind."

Leonardo refused to choose just one path.
Refused to limit himself to a single interest.
And that diversity became his legacy.

So if your interests scatter…
If your curiosity pulls you everywhere at once…
If you've been told to focus on one thing…
Think of Leonardo da Vinci.

He didn't colour inside the lines.
He questioned why the lines existed.
And by thinking differently,
he sketched a future for us all.

Whoopi Goldberg

~ THE STAR WHO FOUND HER
VOICE ONSTAGE ~

Reading sent Whoopi Goldberg into a panic.
At school, the letters danced on the page.
Words refused to stay still.
The harder she tried,
the further they seemed to slip away.

Teachers mistook struggle for laziness.
They accused her of not trying.
Of not paying attention.
Of wasting her potential.

Whoopi is neurodivergent.
Dyslexia.
A brain that learned differently.

School had only one definition of learning.
And Whoopi didn't fit.

But she understood things
the page never could.
She felt rhythm in her body.
Timing in her bones.
Emotion arrived whole,
without needing instruction.

She could become someone else
in a single breath.
Not pretending.
Transforming.

At home, imagination became shelter.
Comedy became armour.
Storytelling became survival.

As a teenager, school felt unbearable.
Every lesson repeated the same quiet lie.
That she didn't belong.

So she left.

To some, it looked like failure.
To Whoopi, it was freedom.

She joined theatre groups.
Trained her voice.
Sharpened her wit.

She built confidence piece by piece.
The kind school never offered.

Then she created something bold.
A one-woman show.
Dozens of characters.
Humour.
Pain.
Truth.
And heart.

Audiences didn't just watch.
They leaned in.
The performance was unlike
anything they'd seen before.

Director Steven Spielberg saw it.
He saw her.

He cast her as Celie in *The Color Purple*.
The role demanded vulnerability.
Depth.
Emotional truth.
Whoopi delivered all of it.

She earned an Academy Award nomination.
And from there, she soared.
She won an Academy Award for *Ghost*.
Became a household name in *Sister Act*.

On television, she spoke up.
As a host on *The View*,
she stood up for the unheard.
The overlooked.

She challenged assumptions.
Spoke openly about dyslexia.

Whoopi once said,

> **"We're here for a reason.
> I believe a bit of the reason is to throw little
> torches out to lead people through the dark."**

So if reading feels hard…
If school makes you doubt yourself…
If your voice feels louder than the page…
Think of Whoopi Goldberg.

She earned an Emmy.
Grammy.
Oscar.
Tony Award.
A rare achievement known as an EGOT.

And proof that school
doesn't get the final say
on who you can become.

Isaac Newton

~ THE THINKER WHO MADE SENSE
OF THE UNIVERSE ~

Isaac Newton was a quiet child.
Not shy.
Just listening.

What held his attention were patterns.
Motion.
Light bending.
Numbers repeating like echoes.

Isaac watched the world closely.
Shadows stretching across the floor.
Sunlight spilling through glass.
Objects falling.
Rolling.
Pausing.
Moving again.

Questions gathered inside him.
Patient.
Persistent.

His mind didn't rush.
It lingered.
Returned.
Focused deeply and stayed there.

Solitude sharpened him.
Crowds drained him.
Small talk dissolved into noise.

At university, Isaac grew restless.
Lectures skimmed the surface.

So he taught himself.

He read endlessly.
Questioned everything.
Filled notebooks with observations.
Calculations.
Sketches.
Questions no one else was asking.

Then the world went quiet.

In 1665, the plague closed universities.
Students were sent home.
Isaac returned to Woolsthorpe.

The silence others feared,
Isaac welcomed.
Quiet meant clarity.

Days stretched.
Thoughts wandered.
Questions stayed long enough to reveal.
And in that stillness,
Isaac's mind caught fire.

The next two years,
ignited the most extraordinary periods
of thinking in human history.

He built the foundations of calculus.
Uncovered the nature of light and colour.
Wrote the laws of motion.
Found gravity.

Not all at once.
But slowly.
Patiently.

The apple story is only part true.
What matters is this:

Isaac saw that the force
pulling fruit to earth
was the same force
guiding planets across the sky.

One rule.
One system.
Everything connected.

For the first time,
the universe made sense.

His ideas became the backbone of science,
explaining how objects move.
How planets orbit.
How invisible forces shape everything we see.

So if you prefer quiet to noise…
If your thoughts deepen when the room empties…
If patterns speak louder than people…
Think of Isaac Newton.

He followed questions into silence.
Where others accepted mystery,
he found structure.

And that quiet boy beneath the apple tree
helped the world understand the universe.

Steven Spielberg

~ THE DIRECTOR WHO SAW STORIES EVERYWHERE ~

Steven Spielberg was the kid
who watched more than he spoke.
The one who stood slightly apart
while the world rushed past.

Noise unsettled him.
Rules felt slippery.

School felt like a place
where he was always behind,
even when he was trying his hardest.

Reading was slow.
Words tangled.

Spelling tests felt unforgiving.
Every mistake loud.
Permanent.

Steven was neurodivergent
with dyslexia.

He didn't think in sentences.
He thought in pictures.
In motion.
In feeling.

He saw stories everywhere.
Shadows stretching across walls.
Light flickering through trees.
The way people moved
when they were scared,
or hopeful,
or alone.

He noticed pauses.
Silences.
The breath before the moment.

His thoughts arrived as scenes.
As camera angles.
As colour and movement.

His imagination was already cinematic
long before he touched a camera.

At twelve, he borrowed his father's camera.
Filmed toy soldiers in the backyard.
Used fireworks for explosions.
Smashed model trains.
Filmed the wreckage.

Again and again.
Take after take.

He directed his friends with certainty.
In his mind, they were already stars.

When he watched the footage back,
he saw it clearly.
He could build worlds.
He could shape emotion.
Film became his language.

But the path forward wasn't easy.
Steven applied to film school.
He was rejected.
Then rejected again.

Each "no" hurt.
But it didn't stop him.

He kept filming.
Kept imagining.
Kept telling stories.

Slowly,
doors opened.
And when they did,
Steven was ready.

Then came the films
that changed cinema forever.

Jaws.
E.T.
Indiana Jones.
Jurassic Park.
Schindler's List.

Steven made audiences feel safe.
Thrilled.
Terrified.
Hopeful.
Sometimes all at once.

He didn't just make movies.
He changed storytelling.

So if reading feels hard…
If your imagination won't sit still…
If your mind tells stories faster than words can follow…
Think of Steven Spielberg.

He proved that the quiet kid
who daydreams today,
can create entirely new worlds tomorrow.

Marie Curie

~ THE SCIENTIST WHO STUDIED IN SECRET~

In Poland, universities were closed to women.
But Marie Curie learned anyway.
In shadows.
In back rooms.
In whispers.

She studied what she wasn't meant to know.
Books stayed when people didn't.
Numbers slowed her breath.
Questions kept her warm.
Learning fed her when food did not.

Marie's focus locked in.
Senses wide open.
Feelings ran deep.
Truth mattered.
So did patterns.

When an idea arrived,
it stayed.
Bright.
Demanding.

Distractions dissolved.
The world blurred.
Truth sharpened.

From Poland to Paris,
life was unforgiving.

Freezing attic rooms.
Cupboards with echoes.
Hunger in her body.
Never in her mind.

She studied through nights
that folded into mornings.
Once absorbed,
hours vanished.
Days blurred.
Time lost its edges.

Marie turned her attention to radiation.
Invisible.
Unstable.
Disobedient.
It refused the rules science trusted.

She stirred boiling chemicals by hand.
Repeated experiments endlessly.
Failed.
Tried again.
Failed better.

The work drained her.
The conditions harmed her.
She continued.

Two elements emerged.
Polonium.
Named for her homeland.
And radium.
Light bleeding from stone.

Marie revealed that atoms
weren't finished things.
Not fixed.
Not final.
They could split.
Change.
Become something new.

Science tilted.
Medicine followed.
Lives changed.

She became the first woman
to win a Nobel Prize.
Then the first person
to win two.

She didn't stop.
She taught.
Researched.
Trained others.
Drove mobile X-ray machines
to wounded soldiers in World War I.

Marie once said,

**"Nothing in life is to be feared.
It is only to be understood."**

Those words guided her work.
And her life.

So if you learn quietly…
If your curiosity ignores permission…
If you're drawn to what others dismiss…
Think of Marie Curie.

She followed questions into darkness.
Trusted her mind.
And by revealing what couldn't be seen,
she changed everything.

Pablo Picasso

~ THE ARTIST WHO CHANGED REALITY ~

Pablo Picasso didn't draw what he saw.
He drew what he felt.
Lines bent and curved.
Faces shifted position.
Perspective fractured.

His mind moved fast.
Fast.
Restless.
Jumping tracks.
But when something held his attention,
everything else fell away.

School felt narrow.
Rules felt final.
One right answer.
One correct way.
That idea never fit him.

But put a pencil in his hand,
or paint,
or charcoal,
or the corner of a napkin,
and the noise softened.
His body settled.
His thoughts ran free.

He could hold many views at once.
Front and side.
Memory and feeling.
Past and present.

Where others saw a cup,
Picasso saw tension.

Collision.
Where others saw a face,
he saw movement.
History still being told.

Reality wasn't stable.
It could bend.
Overlap.
Argue with itself.

As a teenager, realism came easily.
Too easily.
It felt like repetition,
not discovery.
Copying instead of creating.

Picasso wanted freedom.
Feeling.
Art that questioned what we see.

So he broke things apart.
Faces split.
Bodies twisted.
Objects fractured.

Colour stopped behaving.
It became bold.
Urgent.
Unapologetically expressive.

This way of seeing became Cubism.
It challenged centuries of tradition.
It changed art forever.

Other artists painted the world as it appeared.
Picasso painted it from everywhere all at once.

It could move quickly between ideas.
Trust instinct over instruction.
Curiosity over comfort.

He once said,

> "Every child is an artist.
> The problem is how to remain an artist
> once we grow up."

Picasso remained that child.
He created more than 20,000 works of art.
Each one carried his signature intensity.
Restless.
Fearless.
Impossible to ignore.

People argued about his work.
Some were confused.
Many were inspired.
But no one could ignore him.

And no one looked at art the same way again.

So if school feels too narrow…
If your ideas refuse to stay inside neat lines…
If you see the world from angles others don't recognise…
Think of Pablo Picasso.

He didn't just change art.
He changed what artists were allowed to do.

He showed that distortion could be truth.
That emotion mattered more than realism.
That you don't need permission.
You only need courage.

Agatha Christie
~ THE WRITER WHO TURNED SILENCE INTO SUSPENSE ~

For Agatha Christie,
the world arrived at full volume.
Too fast.
Too crowded.

Noise unsettled her.
Crowds drained her.
So she stood back.
Watched.
Listened.

She caught what others missed.
The pause before a reply.
A smile that landed late.
A hand that trembled just enough
to betray a secret.

Agatha's mind ran quietly.
Precisely.
Letters slipped when she wrote.
Spelling resisted order.

Teachers mistook her silence for emptiness.
But inside her,
stories were already overflowing.

She didn't see people
as they wished to be seen.

She saw what lived underneath.
Motives hiding in manners.
Truth tucked into routine.

She spoke less.
Observed more.
Remembered everything.

During World War I,
Agatha trained as a nurse.
Hospitals became classrooms.

She learned about medicines.
Poisons.
Dosage.
Consequence.

She learned what fear does to skin.
How guilt leaks through posture.
How lies fracture under time.
How truth slips out in tiny moments.

Agatha's mind stored it all.

Then she wrote.
Not loudly.
Not quickly.
But deliberately.
Clue by clue.

She created detectives who noticed.
Who listened.
Who trusted observation over force.

Stories that didn't chase violence.
They chased truth.

She asked readers to slow down.
To look.
And then look again.

Agatha once wrote,

"Very few of us are what we seem."

That idea lived at the heart
of every mystery she wrote.

Despite struggling with spelling,
she wrote more than sixty novels.
Hundreds of short stories.
She created *The Mousetrap*,
the longest-running play in history.

Her books sold billions of copies.
Crossed generations.
Languages.
Continents.

Only Shakespeare and the Bible
have reached more readers.

So if silence suits you…
If reading takes effort…
If details cling to you…
Think of Agatha Christie.

She didn't shout to be heard.
She paid attention.
She listened.

And the world waited for what she'd write next.

EXPLORE THESE TITLES
AND MORE

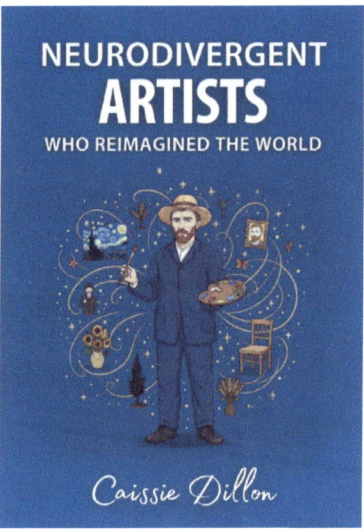

www.neurodivergentlegends.com

About the Author

Caissie Dillon is an Australian storyteller. She has built a career performing on stages, shaping words and ideas for business, and writing for voices that are too often misunderstood or overlooked.

As a neurodivergent person and parent of a neurodivergent child, Caissie understands the beauty and complexity of minds that work differently.

She views neurodivergence not as something to be fixed, but as something to be understood, honoured, and celebrated.

Caissie writes for children and young adults who feel out of place, for families and educators learning new language around how minds can work, and for anyone beginning to realise that what makes them different may also be what makes them extraordinary.

www.ingramcontent.com/pod-product-compliance
Lightning Source LLC
Chambersburg PA
CBHW042258280426
43661CB00097BA/1183